Bristol Port and Channel Nostalgia

by

Malcolm Cranfield

An unusual ship for Bristol Steam Navigation's short sea services, the **Sappho** was built at Goole in 1949 and had previously traded as the Swedish **Falster**, owned by A/S Ferm, a company created in 1881 and part of the Broström Group. She was purchased by the Bristol company in 1960 but was as infrequent caller at Bristol's City Docks. Photographed sailing from Avonmouth on 1 October 1964, **Sappho** was sold to Canada in 1966 to become **Ghislain-Marie**, a name shortened to **Ghislain** in 1967. Resold within Canada in 1970, she initially traded as **Anik** but sailed between 1971 and 1973 as **Maya** under the Cayman Islands flag. She is reported to have been scrapped in about 1976 as **Anik**.

INTRODUCTION

It was easy in the early 1960s for a teenager living at Portishead to acquire an interest in shipping. Almost every tide brought a variety of ships passing Battery Point while visits to Avonmouth Docks, using the ferry across the River Avon between Pill and Shirehampton, provided a fascinating new dimension. This book is a pictorial record of some of the ships seen during the ten years from 1964 to 1974, by which time the trade of Bristol Port began to decline. The ships range from those owned locally, by well-known British lines and by a variety of foreign operators. Histories of the ships and their owners are provided together with information on the trading which had brought them to the port.

Before the internet there were elements of surprise and eager anticipation based upon lists of "ships expected" published in the *Western Daily Press*, *Lloyd's List* or the Port of Bristol Authority's internal daily and weekly lists. Visits and telephone calls to the ever helpful Dockmaster's Office and shipping agents, whose advice and experience were much appreciated, became a necessity in later years. The presence of tugs waiting off Avonmouth was the best indicator that something was expected: normally two tugs for a dry cargo ship or three for a tanker; tugs waiting off Portishead dock indicated an arrival into Avonmouth late on the tide or possibly a ship bound for Portishead, Bristol City docks or Sharpness. A ship's destination was usually indicated by two pennants identifying the dock for which it was bound: Royal Edward Dock (blue and yellow), Avonmouth Old Dock (red and white) or Portishead dock. Ships heading for Bristol City docks did not fly pennants while the presence of the Sharpness pilot boat was an obvious clue. Avonmouth's lockside docking signal, the lower of two black balls being lowered when the lock was ready for an inward ship, indicated whether the next movement was inward or outward. Ships sailing from Sharpness passed Portishead late on the ebb tide. The presence at Battery Point of a lookout, erected for war time use, provided shelter in all weathers while waiting.

The photographs at Avonmouth, mainly of ships arriving or sailing from the Royal Edward Dock, were taken from either of the two piers. The south pier was the location used between the wars by a photographer whose easily recognisable and well-known work can be seen in many shipping publications. I feel privileged to have followed in his footsteps, encouraged by mentors such as the late Des Harris, Alex Duncan and Laurence Dunn, the journey shared with good friend Graham Thursby and with many other like-minded friends met along the way.

Malcolm Cranfield - September, 2013

Published by Bernard McCall, 400 Nore Road, Portishead, Bristol, BS20 8EZ, England. Website: www.coastalshipping.co.uk
Telephone/fax: 01275 846178 E-mail: bernard@coastalshipping.co.uk All distribution enquiries should be addressed to the publisher.

Printed by Amadeus Press, Ezra House, West 26 Business Park, Cleckheaton, West Yorkshire, BD19 4TQ, England. Website: www.amadeuspress.co.uk
Telephone: 01274 863210 Fax: 01274 863211 E-mail: info@amadeuspress.co.uk

ISBN: 978-1-902953-61-8.

Front cover: **Butegarth**, built at Lowestoft and delivered to Rea Towing at Cardiff in January 1966, had been ordered to Avonmouth to assist on the busy afternoon tide of 11 March 1968. The Bulgarian **Adhara** had also arrived in the Bristol Channel that day but, due to the port's busy programme, was unable to dock, turning around off Walton Bay before returning to Breaksea anchorage to await the following tide. Sold in 1990 to become **Avoca**, **Butegarth** was soon resold to operate at Lisbon as **Lutamar**. The East German **Bernhard Bastlein**, assisted by C J King's tug **Sea Queen**, was photographed rounding Avonmouth's north pier with cargo loaded at Kakinada and Bombay on a voyage which had started at the Bangladesh jute port of Chalna on 20 January, completing at Rostock on 31 March, with calls at Leixões (Portugal), Avonmouth, London, Antwerp and Bremen. **Sea Queen**, built in 1944 as **Empire Walter** and purchased by King in 1946, was later sold to Spanish breakers, arriving at Gijon in June 1974.

Back cover: P & A Campbell's paddle steamer **Bristol Queen** was built in Bristol in 1946. She made a fine sight as she passed Battery Point on the morning of 8 June 1964. White Funnel ships made a good contribution to the war effort, including the Dunkirk evacuation, but with the loss of most of the fleet. The post-war era ushered in a period of ambition with the building of **Bristol Queen** and also, at Glasgow, the **Cardiff Queen**. Launched at Charles Hill's shipyard on 4 April 1946 using a bottle of Harvey's Bristol Milk, **Bristol Queen** was unfortunately laid up for several seasons in the 1950s and, suffering frequent machinery problems, collided with Penarth pier in fog in August 1966. She damaged a paddle wheel a year later and suffered a collision at Cardiff on 14 January 1968. She was then sold for breaking at Willebroek, south of Antwerp.

British India Steam Navigation's "school ship" **Devonia** is seen sailing from Avonmouth on 2 May 1966. Launched as **Devonshire** for Bibby Line on 20 December 1938, she was completed in July 1939 as a troopship with capacity for 250 passengers and 1150 troops. Leaving Southampton on 11 August 1939, **Devonshire** was equipped with landing craft and in 1942 carried assault craft to the Salerno and D-Day landings. She subsequently served in the Malayan campaign and Korean War. Refitted by her builders, Fairfield at Govan in 1953 she returned to trooping duties until her charter to the Ministry of Transport ended in 1961. After purchase by British India in January 1962, as **Devonia**, she was converted for educational cruising by Barclay Curle at Whiteinch, Glasgow. Joining **Dunera** (built in 1937), **Devonia** voyaged mainly to the Mediterranean and Baltic Sea until sold for breaking at La Spezia in December 1967, to be replaced by **Uganda**.

We must include a photograph of Bristol City Line's steamship **Bristol City**. She was built in 1959 at the Readhead shipyard in South Shields. We see her passing Portishead, inbound for Avonmouth, on 28 September 1968 at the end of a routine North Atlantic crossing. On 31 August 1970 she sailed from Avonmouth as **Agelos Gabriel** under the new ownership of Christos Lemos but still in Bristol City L0ine colours, bound for Barry for painting and repairs, eventually sailing on 21 October bound for China. As **Agelos Gabriel**, she traded worldwide until laid up at Chalkis on 17 June 1977 and, after almost three years idle, moving to Split in Yugoslavia for breaking, arriving on 3 April 1980. Bristol City Line was part of a company with shipbuilding and ship repairing interests which was founded in 1879 by Charles Hill who had taken over the business from George Hillhouse in 1845. Bristol City Line initially traded to east coast USA, starting a service to Canada in 1933 which was extended to the Great Lakes in 1958.

The **Gloucester City** was an earlier product of the Readhead yard built for Bristol City Line. She was built in 1954 and had a sistership named **New York City**. We see **Gloucester City** near the end of her career, outbound from Avonmouth, on 23 February 1967. On 25 May 1968 she sailed from Avonmouth under the Liberian flag but Greek ownership as **St John** as which she was sadly wrecked at Fort Dauphin, Madagascar, on 30 October that year during a voyage from Montreal to Djakarta. Links had meantime been forged with Bibby Line who in 1966 took a 22% stake

in Bristol City Line and built two new ships, **Toronto City** and **Coventry City**, for operation on the North Atlantic. With Bibby doubtless providing finance for the purchase of ships and containers, Bristol City Line proceeded to enter the container age in 1969 by creating Dart Container Line in partnership with CMB of Belgium and Clarke Traffic Services of Canada. In February 1971 Bibby took a 51% stake in Bristol City Line whose independent cargo liner services then soon ceased.

The Bristol City Line was not unique in using names ending "City". Sir William Reardon Smith's **Houston City** was built at the Wm Doxford yard in Sunderland in 1963. Registered in Bideford, she is seen arriving at Avonmouth on 3 March 1966 at the end of a long voyage from Kitimat via Stockton (California), Oakland, Long Beach, Guaymas, San Jose (Costa Rica), Champerico (Guatamala), Acajutla (El Salvador), Corinto (Nicaragua), Cristobal, Leixoes, Le Havre, Dunkirk and Rotterdam. **Houston City**, together with sistership **Cardiff City**, was sold in 1972 to Wm Brandts (Fourth Leasing) Ltd for leasing to Transportacion Maritima Mexicana ("TMM") of Mexico as operator, Reardon Smith remaining as manager. Renamed **Maria Elisa**, she was sold on in 1980, together with sistership **Sara Lupe**, to the Hong Kong-based John McRink who traded the ships as **Alpac Africa** and **Alpac Asia** respectively. The former **Houston City** finally arrived at Shanghai in July 1984 to be broken up. The firm of Reardon Smith, founded at Cardiff in 1905, ceased trading in 1985.

No engines were being used as the **Suevic** moved from a lay by berth in the oil basin to a working berth at Avonmouth on 21 October 1972. The ship was built in 1950 for Shaw, Savill & Albion by Harland & Wolff at Belfast. She was eventually sold to breakers, arriving at Kaohsiung on 6 June 1974. While the Albion Line had started business at Glasgow in 1856, Robert Shaw and Walter Savill, employed in London by shipbrokers in the New Zealand trade, had formed Shaw, Savill & Co in 1858. The combined Shaw, Savill & Albion Line was created in 1882. From 1884 to 1933 it ran a joint service to New Zealand together with the Oceanic Steam Navigation Company's White Star Line, holding company for Lord Kylsant's empire. In 1933 control of Shaw, Savill & Albion was acquired by Furness, Withy & Co while White Star Line passed to Cunard. It is interesting to note that Shaw, Savill & Albion continued to use White Star-style names with the suffix "-ic".

The **California Star** with 421,000 cubic feet of refrigerated capacity was built by Harland & Wolff at Belfast in 1945 as **Empire Clarendon**. She became **Tuscan Star** in 1947, **Timaru Star** in 1948 and **California Star** in 1958. We see her passing Portishead on 2 August 1964. **California Star** arrived at Kaohsiung on 21 April 1969 to be broken up after a plan to convert her into a fish factory ship failed to materialise. A sistership, **Empire Abercorn**, purchased in 1946 by the New Zealand Shipping Company Limited, traded as **Rakaia** until broken up at Hong Kong in 1971.

The **Wellington Star** was built for Blue Star Line by John Brown at Clydebank in 1952. We see her passing Portishead on 12 September 1967. She had sailed from Opua on 21 July 1967 and had also called at Liverpool and London. **Wellington Star** was sold at Sydney in October 1975 to Abbas Gokal's Gulf Shipping Group and renamed **Hawkes Bay**. As such she then largely traded between Australia and the Arabian Gulf, having been slightly modified for the carriage of livestock. **Hawkes Bay** arrived at Kaohsiung on 9 August 1979 to be broken up. Blue Star Line

was the creation of the Vestey family who had cattle ranching and meat processing interests in South America. After using Royal Mail Steam Packet Company services in the late 19th century, and then in the early 20th century chartering ships, Blue Star Line was created in 1911 for the carriage of frozen meat from South America in their own ships. The company, which traded from Australia and New Zealand from 1933, was sold in 1998 to P&O Nedlloyd.

Blue Funnel Line's **Cyclops** was photographed in clear winter conditions passing Portishead, inbound for Avonmouth, on 14 February 1970 at the end of another voyage from the Far East. This was on a particularly busy tide as the entrance lock had been out of commission under repair for several days beforehand. **Cyclops**, built by Scott's at Greenock in 1948, was an example of many ships ordered after World War Two by Alfred Holt's Ocean SS Company ("Blue Funnel Line"). Known as the "A" Class, **Cyclops** and five others were designated "Mark 2". In July 1975, she was renamed **Automedon** to release the name **Cyclops** for a new tanker and in December that year was transferred to Elder Dempster Line services but was soon sold for breaking, arriving at Dalmuir on the Clyde on 25 August 1977.

Alfred Holt's "Victory" ship **Tantalus** was photographed passing Portishead, following an overnight snowfall on the morning of 9 December 1967 during a voyage from Shanghai, from where she had sailed on 9 September, to Liverpool, Dublin, Avonmouth and Newport. Built at Richmond, California, in 1945 as **Macmurray Victory**, she was one of a number of war-built ships purchased by British lines to replace lost tonnage. Acquired by Alfred Holt's Blue Funnel Line in 1946 she was renamed **Polyphemus** and then **Tantalus** in 1960. Laid up at Falmouth in March 1969, she finally sailed on 14 October as **Pelops** bound for Durban and then Kaohsiung where she arrived for breaking on New Year's Day 1970. In 1865 Alfred and Philip Holt of Liverpool, intending to

operate steamships which could compete with the sailing ships in the China trade, had taken delivery of three new steam ships from Scott's of Greenock. Named **Agamemnon**, **Ajax** and **Achilles**, so began the Ocean Steam Ship Company which became the best known shipping line in the Far East trade. Following the formation of Overseas Containers Limited (OCL) in 1965, 1967 saw a major restructuring, and by 1978 nearly 90% of the Far East trade was containerised. The Blue Funnel fleet was reduced to a few ships operating in joint services with Ben Line and Barber Lines and Ocean's involvement with deep sea shipping finally came to an end in 1989.

Blue Funnel Line's **Deucalion** was memorably seen on 20 April 1971 outbound from Avonmouth where, after calls at Glasgow and Liverpool, she had completed loading cargo for the Far East before being broken up at Kaohsiung where she arrived on 9 June 1971. This was the last outward Blue Funnel call at Avonmouth. **Deucalion** was in reality a Glen Line ship, the 1939 Dundee-built **Glengyle** which had been renamed just a few months earlier, in October 1970, on being transferred to Alfred Holt's Ocean SS Company ahead of her previous round trip to the Far East on the Blue Funnel berth. On delivery in 1939, **Glengyle** was taken over by the Admiralty and converted into a fast supply ship as **HMS Glengyle**. Modified in 1940 for carrying infantry to support commando raids, she had a varied wartime career, taking part in the Anzio landings in January 1944 before sailing to India and the Far East, in 1946 evacuating British prisoners of war from Subic Bay to the Clyde. Returned to Glen Line, she was refitted for commercial operations by Vickers Armstrong at Newcastle, rejoining the fleet in March 1948. Glen Line had entered the China tea trade using steam ships following the opening of the Suez Canal in 1869. Glen Line Ltd, formed in 1910, in 1920 amalgamated with the Shire Line. In 1935, following the "Kylsant crash", Glen and Shire Lines were taken over by Alfred Holt, from 1972 together a part of Ocean Transport & Trading. Traditionally, Alfred Holt's Blue Funnel Line ships had loaded at west coast UK ports while Glen & Shire Lines served east coast UK ports but from 1974, together with Ben Line, they jointly served all UK ports within Ben-Ocean Services. Faced with increasing containerisation of the Far East trade, this however survived only until 1978 when the last Glen Line ship was sold.

Blue Funnel Line's **Memnon** is passing Portishead on 26 February 1970 outbound from Avonmouth where she had completed loading cargo for the Far East. Normally a discharge port, an experiment with loading cargo at Avonmouth, possibly due to industrial problems at Liverpool, was short-lived. Following a brief time charter to Safmarine in 1974, **Memnon** was transferred to the South East Asia - Australia service in 1975 and renamed **Stentor**. Returning to the UK in 1977 for use on Elder Dempster Lines' services to West Africa, she was later renamed **Owerri** but soon sold in June 1978 to European Navigation Inc (Captain S Karnessis and Mrs D Vlassakis) of Piraeus, and renamed **Europe**. The same buyers also purchased sistership **Opobo** (ex **Rhexenor**, ex **Maron**) and renamed her **Europe II**. Both ships spent most of 1981 in Angola and returned to Piraeus in March/April 1982 only to lay up. The former **Memnon** moved to Stylis in July 1982 for that purpose. After lying idle for five years, they were sold for breaking in 1987. **Europe II** was demolished at Aliaga, Turkey while **Europe**, the former **Memnon**, sailed as **Primus** for Alang, India, where she was beached in February 1988.

Clan Line's **Clan Macgregor**, built at Greenock in 1962, made an impressive sight passing close to Portishead at speed bound for Avonmouth on the afternoon tide of 28 December 1971. She had sailed from Madras on 6 November for Avonmouth, Dublin and Liverpool. On 31 December 1955, Clan Line and Union Castle Line (including King Line and Bullard King & Company) merged to form British & Commonwealth. While British & Commonwealth had in 1969 invested in Overseas Containers Limited (OCL), Clan Line continued to operate to India and

East and South Africa but ceased to exist on the sale of **Clan Alpine**, **Clan Macgillivray** and **Clan Macgregor** in 1981. **Clan Macgregor**, nominally owned by King Line between 1969 and 1977, was the last ship to be owned by Clan Line, sold to become **Angelika R** at the end of 1981. Owned by Dedalos Cia Nav SA of Athens, she suffered an engine room fire off Cyprus on 9 November 1982 and in March 1983 was towed via Piraeus to Laurium on the southern Greek mainland where she was broken up.

Clan Macleod had sailed for Avonmouth from Visakhapatnam, India, on 8 July 1967, just one month after the closure of the Suez Canal following the "Six Day War". This event led to extended voyage durations until the Canal reopened in June 1975. The origins of Clan Line go back to 1877 when C W Cayzer & Company commenced business in Liverpool, trading from the UK to India. The company, which became Cayzer, Irvine & Company in 1878 when Captain William Irvine joined the firm, became the manager of Clan Line while also acting as a vehicle for the acquisition of other companies. In 1881 the Clan Line Association of Steamers was formed and the company was moved to Glasgow. Built at Greenock, launched on 13 February 1948 and completed in July 1948, ***Clan Macleod*** was photographed entering Avonmouth's Royal Edward lock on 9 September 1967. She was sold to Pakistani principals in 1976 and renamed ***Papaji*** as which she was beached near Karachi in November 1977 to be broken up.

Ellerman Hall Line's *City of Ottawa* sails past Portishead against the incoming tide on Christmas Eve 1970 bound for Liverpool from Bombay after discharging a part cargo at Avonmouth. Her next outward voyage was from Glasgow to Beira under the new name of *City of Leeds*. Hall Line, founded in 1868 as Sun Shipping by Robert Alexander, a Belfast-born but Liverpool-based shipbroker, had concentrated on the India trade, with Bombay as its main port. Sold to Ellerman in 1901, Hall Line had developed into South and East Africa as well as holding its own in the competitive Indian trade untl succumbing to the growth of the Indian national lines and, later, containerisation. The *City of Ottawa* was a 15.5 knot motorship built by Vickers Armstrong at Newcastle. She was launched on 19 January 1950 and completed in August 1950. As *City of Leeds* she was sold in 1975 to the London and Hong Kong-based, Karachi-domiciled Gulf Shipping Group. Renamed *Gulf Venture*, she finally arrived at Gadani Beach in November 1977 to be broken up.

Ellerman & Bucknall's *City of Pretoria* was built in 1947 by Cammell Laird at Birkenhead. She made a glorious sight sailing from Avonmouth on the afternoon of 4 November 1965. Ellerman Lines had, in 1908, acquired Bucknall Steamship Lines which had operated between the UK, South Africa and also North America and Australasia. The Ellerman & Bucknall Steamship Company was created in 1914, retaining a separate identity until merged into Ellerman City Liners in 1973. In 1985 Ellerman was purchased by its management from the Barclay Brothers, owners since 1983, who then sold to Trafalgar House. In 1987 the operation was merged with Cunard Line to form Cunard-Ellerman. Acquired in 1991 by Andrew Weir Shipping, the former Ellerman services were sold to Hamburg Süd at the end of 2002 and the Ellerman name ceased to be used. After a final voyage from East Africa, *City of Pretoria* sailed from Liverpool early in 1967 bound for Japanese shipbreakers. She had been renamed *Proxeneion* and arrived at Izumiohtsu on 18 May 1967.

Rubens was photographed passing Battery Point outbound from Avonmouth on 8 June 1971 after discharging a cargo from the River Plate area of South America. Built by Wm Pickersgill at Sunderland in 1951 as *Crispin* for Booth Line, she took the name **Mandowi** in 1953 for Austasia Line service before reverting to Booth Line as **Dunstan** in 1966 and then becoming **Rubens** in 1967, managed by Lamport & Holt and operating on their services. Sold by the Vestey Group in 1973 to the Greek shipowner George Kalogeras and renamed **Irini K**, she was very soon sold for breaking and beached at Istanbul on 24 April 1974 for that purpose. Lamport & Holt Line derived from an 1845 partnership involving George Holt whose brother Alfred spent a short period with Lamport and Holt

before founding his own shipping company, Alfred Holt & Company, the Blue Funnel Line. Trading primarily to the River Plate, Lamport & Holt was acquired in 1911 by Lord Kylsant's competing Royal Mail Group but, following the "Kylsant crash", again traded independently until purchased in 1944 by the Vestey Group's Blue Star Line. Alfred Booth had meanwhile started trading in 1866 to northern Brazil and the Amazon, founding Booth Steamship Company in 1881. Purchased in 1946 by the Vestey Group, the management of the three companies was thereafter closely interwoven. In 1974 Blue Star Ship Management was created to manage the joint Vestey Group fleets.

Lamport & Holt Line's **Roland** was photographed arriving at Avonmouth on 10 March 1973, again with a cargo from the River Plate area of South America. **Roland**, ordered from A Stephen & Sons at Glasgow by Lancashire Shipping Company and launched on 18 April 1950 as **Bolton Castle**, was delivered to Blue Star Line in September 1950 as **Dunedin Star**, having been given a larger funnel size to match the Blue Star image. Lancashire Shipping Company's Castle Line had in 1944 been acquired by Mollers of Hong Kong who had intended after the war ended to resume a joint service with Barber Steamship Lines of New York and Wilh Wilhelmsen of Oslo but, after ordering three new ships including **Bolton Castle**, withdrew from the agreement and sold the ship on the stocks. **Dunedin Star** was transferred to Lamport & Holt Line in 1968, operating as **Roland** between Europe and South America until sold at Liverpool in mid 1975. Renamed **Jessica**, she finally arrived at Gadani Beach on 10 June 1978 to be broken up.

Royal Mail Lines' **Loch Gowan** was photographed from Avonmouth's north pier on 13 February 1965 as she approached the port on a voyage from Vancouver. Built in 1954 by Harland & Wolff at Belfast, she arrived at Kaohsiung on 28 March 1970 to be broken up. Royal Mail Lines Limited was formed in 1932 after the collapse of the Kylsant shipping group, taking over the assets of the Royal Mail Steam Packet Company, the Nelson Line and David MacIver & Company. Royal Mail Lines was itself taken over in 1965 by Furness, Withy & Company and some ships were thereafter interchanged between the fleets operated by Royal Mail, Shaw, Savill & Albion, Pacific Steam Navigation and Furness Withy. **Loch Gowan**'s last voyages were to the west coast of South America on the Pacific Steam Navigation service.

Royal Mail Lines' **Essequibo** passes Portishead, outbound from Avonmouth, on 6 November 1965 after discharging a cargo of sulphur from Beaumont. She was bound for Liverpool to load again for the west coast of South America on Pacific Steam Navigation service. Built in 1952 by Harland & Wolff at Glasgow, **Essequibo** was sold in 1968 to trade under China Navigation ownership as **Ningpo** until 1970 and then as the Burmese **Kalewa** until finally arriving at Shanghai on 15 March 1976 to be broken up. Queen Victoria had in 1839 granted a Royal Charter to the newly-formed Royal Mail Steam Packet Company to carry mail to the West Indies and Caribbean. Under the management of Lord Kylsant in the early 20th century, the Royal Mail Group acquired several other shipping lines including, in 1927, the White Star Line, but soon afterwards went bankrupt. Pacific Steam Navigation was linked with Royal Mail Lines from 1910 until 1984 when both names disappeared within the Furness Withy Group.

Port Brisbane, passing Portishead on the evening tide of 30 September 1970, was bound for Glasgow to load cargo for Auckland and New Plymouth. Her inward voyage was from Whangarei, New Zealand, sailing on 19 May 1970 for London, Southampton, Belfast and finally Avonmouth. Built in 1949 by Swan, Hunter and Wigham Richardson at Wallsend, **Port Brisbane** finally arrived at Hong Kong on 2 November 1975 to be broken up. William Milburn had introduced the "Port" naming policy in 1883 with the creation of the Anglo-Australian Steam Navigation Company. The Port Line name evolved after 1916 when, in order to diversify, the Cunard Steamship Company bought what had by then become the Commonwealth & Dominion Line. Renamed Cunard Line Australasian Services, the company became Port Line Limited in 1937.

With increased reefer capacity, the 15 knot **Port Lyttelton**, built for Port Line by Hawthorn, Leslie at Newcastle in 1947, was an improved version of the war-built **Port Macquarie** and **Port Lincoln**. Said by one crew member to be a "happy ship and good feeder", **Port Lyttelton**, however, suffered a grounding off Florida in 1953 and serious engine problems while at Brisbane in 1959. She is seen sailing past Portishead on 13 September 1967 on a positioning voyage to the UK from Hampton Roads on the east coast of the United States. These ships had normally traded between the east coast of Canada/USA and Australasia on the Montreal - Australia - New Zealand (MANZ) Line service, a joint venture started in 1936 between Port Line, Ellerman & Bucknall and the New Zealand Shipping Company to link Australia and New Zealand with Montreal and eastern Canada which was later extended to the United States.

One of a series of ships built by Wm Hamilton at Port Glasgow, launched on 24 June 1948 and completed in November 1948, the **Mahseer** had a service speed of 15 knots. She made a nostalgic sight passing Portishead outbound from Avonmouth in the early morning of 12 November 1968 after discharging a part cargo from India. Essentially founded in Massachusetts in 1770 by Daniel Brocklebank of Whitehaven, the firm of Thos & Jno Brocklebank, created at his home town in 1801, moved to Liverpool in 1819. In 1911 Brocklebank's shares were sold to members of the Cunard board of directors, who also purchased the whole of the ordinary share capital of Anchor Line, and in 1912 a joint service to Calcutta was formed, known as Anchor-Brocklebank which lasted until 1935. **Mahseer** was the most long-lived of Brocklebank's several post-war newbuildings, surviving the pooling of the fleet with Cunard in 1968 but finally scrapped near Karachi where she was beached on 16 June 1975. The Indian service ended with the sale of **Mahronda** and **Manipur** in 1977 and Brocklebank ceased trading in 1983 after operating former Port Line ships on non-Indian services between 1975 and 1983.

Outbound from Avonmouth on 4 March 1967, Brocklebank's **Mathura** had commenced loading cargo at Chalna and Calcutta at the end of December, reportedly bound for London, Manchester and Liverpool. Her call at Avonmouth may therefore have been an unscheduled diversion from London. The **Mathura** was powered by steam turbines and had a service speed of 16 knots. She was the last of five sisterships built by Wm Hamilton at Glasgow, having been launched on 7 September 1959 and completed in January 1960. Laid up at Falmouth in August 1971, she was sold to Marchessini Lines in March 1972 and renamed **Eurytion**. Trading on a liner service between Europe, the United States and Far East, she was resold in 1977 to Kuwaiti principals who named her **Alwaha**. On her first voyage bound for Turkey, **Alwaha** suffered boiler trouble, an engine room fire and water ingress, putting into Aden for refuge. She was eventually sold to breakers, sailing under tow of the tug **Irishman** for Karachi where she anchored off in October 1978 only to suffer a collision before finally being beached at Gadani Beach in March 1979.

Owned by Charente Steamship (T & J Harrison of Liverpool), the steam turbine powered **Forester** was built at the Readhead shipyard in South Shields. Launched in December 1951 and delivered in May 1952 she passes Portishead on 2 March 1968 outbound from Avonmouth on a voyage from East Africa. Harrisons, who had started business with brigs engaged in the wine trade, mainly from the River Charente in France, in 1857 purchased their first iron ship, **Philosopher**, forming the Charente Steamship Company in 1884 with Thos and Jas Harrison as managers.

Over the years, the company's services were extended to the Caribbean and United States Gulf, India and East and South Africa with those to the Caribbean lasting longest, between 1978 and 1998 in a joint service with CGM, the French Line, but the company was too small to survive in the age of containerisation and, in October 2000, sold its remaining business to P & O Nedlloyd. **Forester** was sold in 1970 to become **Maldive Ambassador** and she arrived at Tadotsu, Japan, on 20 October 1973 to be broken up.

Harrison Line's **Custodian** was built by Wm Doxford at Sunderland in 1961. Only the second Harrison ship, after the **Adventurer**, to be equipped with a Stülcken heavy lift derrick, we see her passing Portishead on 28 January 1969. Sold to Greece in 1979 to become **Sea Pearl** under the ownership of Thenamaris Maritime, in 1981 she was resold to Mighty Management SA (G Doussopoulos and Vas Maltezos) and renamed **Mighty Pearl**. She ran aground on 2 February 1982, south-east of Inagua Island in the Bahamas after suffering engine trouble during a loaded voyage from Montreal to Kingston in Jamaica. The tug **Fairplay IX** attempted to refloat her but, having been holed in three separate places with her engine room flooded, **Mighty Pearl** was eventually abandoned to insurance underwriters.

Anchor Line's **Caledonia** had arrived in the Bristol Channel late on the day tide of 20 August 1965, intending to dock at Avonmouth while there was sufficient water but, due to the delayed sailing of **Trevalgan**, the docking was abandoned and she was photographed passing Portishead Point returning to Breaksea anchorage to await the following tide. **Caledonia** eventually sailed five days later from Avonmouth to Liverpool to load out for Bombay for the last time. The **Caledonia** was built by the Fairfield shipyard at Govan on the River Clyde, launched on 12 March 1947 and completed on 23 March 1948. Together with **Cilicia** and **Circassia**, she was built for Anchor Line's Glasgow to New York service. The ship was sold late in 1965 for use as a floating hostel for students at Amsterdam where she lay from December 1965 until broken up at Harburg, Hamburg, in 1971. The Glasgow-based Handysides & Henderson partnership had started Anchor Line services between Glasgow, Liverpool and Bombay in 1875. Anchor Line, although purchased by Cunard in 1911, retained its separate identity and management, in 1912 entering a joint Anchor-Brocklebank service to India and in 1916 forming a joint Anchor-Donaldson Line to operate the passenger service to Canada while participating in a joint sailing schedule with Cunard. Anchor Line was liquidated in 1935 but finance was injected by Runciman Limited of Newcastle. Between 1949 and 1953, United Molasses Co had gained control of the company but, after United Molasses Co became a subsidiary of Tate & Lyle in 1965, Anchor Line was sold to Runciman whose Moor Line ships were in 1968 transferred to Anchor Line for operation on the Indian services. On the sale of the former Moor Line ships in 1976, Anchor Line took ships on voyage charters for outward loading from the UK to India until closing operations at the end of the 1980s as containerisation took hold.

Passing Portishead on 24 August 1966 outbound from Avonmouth with a part cargo for discharge at Liverpool, **Inchdouglas** was on a voyage charter to Anchor Line. She had sailed from Bedi Bunder, Gujarat, India, on 11 July 1966. Built at Sunderland as **Jersey Hart** to a standard Doxford design, she was launched on 20 December 1942 and delivered to Morel Shipping of Cardiff in May 1943. She became Stanhope Shipping's **Stanpark** in 1945, Thomas Dunlop's **Queen Eleanor** in 1951 and Douglas Steamship Company's **Inchdouglas** in 1956. Douglas Steamship Company had been formed in Hong Kong in 1883 by Douglas Lapraik. On the death in 1950 of S T Williamson, who in 1932 had bought a controlling interest in the company, J R Mullion took control but sold the remaining two ships due to difficult trading conditions. However, in 1956 three former Empire ships were purchased, of which **Inchdouglas** was one, from 1966 formally managed by Mullion & Co. In 1969-1970 the Empire-type ships were replaced by newer tonnage and **Inchdouglas** was sold to Taiwan breakers, arriving at Kaohsiung in November 1970.

British India Steam Navigation's **Orna**, seen on 13 October 1967, was also on a voyage charter to Anchor Line from Karachi and Bedi Bunder. The corporate origins of British India can be traced back to The Calcutta & Burmah Steam Navigation Company, created in Glasgow in 1856 to trade along the Indian coast. Expansion in services towards the Persian Gulf and South East Asia led the company's owner, William Mackinnon, to float the British India SN Company Limited which was registered in Scotland on 28 October 1862. James Lyle Mackay, latterly the first Earl of Inchcape, responsible for the merger of the P&O and British India SN in 1914, had ensured the continued corporate identity of British India SN until 1971 when the P&O Group was reorganised. **Orna**, with a service speed of only 11.5 knots, was built by Barclay, Curle at Glasgow in 1938 for both cargo and passenger services in the East, rarely visiting the United Kingdom. **Orna** arrived at Hong Kong on 12 March 1969 to be broken up.

Elder Dempster Lines' **Kaduna**, passing Portishead on 2 November 1965 at the end of a voyage from West Africa, had been built by Lithgows at Port Glasgow in 1956 for the British & Burmese Steam Navigation Company (P Henderson) and had only recently been transferred within the Ocean Steamship Group following its acquisition of Henderson Line. Alexander Elder and John Dempster were, in the second half of the 19th century, agents in Liverpool for the British and African Steam Navigation Company. In 1900 Alfred Lewis Jones, who had joined them in 1879, acquired a majority share of the competing African Steamship Company, propelling Elder Dempster into the main shipowner serving West Africa. On the death of Alfred Jones in 1909, Lord Kylsant took control but after the collapse of his Royal Mail Group in 1931 Elder Dempster Lines was managed by its major shareholder, Alfred Holt's Ocean Steamship Company. **Kaduna**, along with sistership **Kumba**, was sold in 1973 to Regent Navigation Corporation, a company linked with Maldives Shipping, and renamed **Regent Reliance**. As such she was beached near Karachi, at Gadani Beach, on 22 April 1978 to be broken up.

Arriving at Avonmouth on 31 March 1966 is Guinea Gulf Line's **Mano**. Dating from 1947, she had been built at Scott's shipyard in Greenock as **Sulima** for Elder Dempster Lines and, along with five sisterships, had only recently been transferred to Guinea Gulf Line on its acquisition by Elder Dempster. **Mano** was sold in 1967 to the London Greek Frangos Brothers and renamed **Anna F**. As such she was laid up at Antwerp with engine damage between May 1972 and September 1973, leaving for Gdansk under tow for intended repairs which were found to be uneconomic. When being towed to breakers at Santander, **Anna F** broke adrift and stranded south of Klaipeda on 4 December 1973.

P&O's **Somali** had sailed from Calcutta on 30 April 1969 on her last inward voyage to the United Kingdom. Photographed arriving at Avonmouth on 12 June, she was soon to be sold to the London Greek owner L Haji Ioannou (Troodos Shipping & Trading) and by October 1969 was reported at Colombo as **Happyland**. The name Peninsular Steam Navigation Company derived from a service started in 1835 between London and the Iberian peninsula. The name of Peninsular and Oriental Steam Navigation Company (P&O) was incorporated in 1840 when a contract was secured to deliver mail to Alexandria. In 1965, P&O, together with Ocean Steamship, Furness Withy and British &

Commonwealth, established Overseas Containers Limited (OCL) and by the early 1980s had converted all of its dry cargo liner routes to container operations. Subsequently becoming P&O Containers Limited (P&OCL) and merging with Nedlloyd in 1996 to form P&O Nedlloyd, the company was in June 2005 purchased by A P Møller and absorbed into the Maersk operation. **Somali**, a 17 knot ship, built by Barclay, Curle at Glasgow to a British India specification, had been launched on 22 April 1948 and was completed in December 1948. As **Happyland**, she arrived at Kaohsiung in September 1972 to be broken up.

Bibby Line's **Herefordshire**, built in 1943 by Barclay, Curle at Whiteinch, Glasgow passes Portishead on 5 May 1967 during a voyage from Burma, a service calling at Egypt and Colombo which Arthur Wilson Bibby had started in 1891 but ended in 1971. **Herefordshire**'s design was similar to a series of ships built by Barclay, Curle for British India and was almost identical to Ellerman's **City of Chester**, completed by the same yard two months later, in March 1944. Between 1954 and 1961, **Herefordshire** had been long term chartered to Port Line, trading as **Port Hardy**, and in 1969 was sold to Troodos Shipping & Trading (L Haji Ioannou) who renamed her **Merryland** as which she arrived at Kaohsiung on 2 February 1973 to be broken up. Bibby Line, unlike most of the other British shipowners mentioned, remains in business as an owner of ships and as a ship management company.

Bibby Line's **Warwickshire** was built in 1948 at the Fairfield yard in Govan. Guided by the tug **Bristolian**, she was photographed leaving Avonmouth on 26 March 1965 during her last voyage from Burma. Together with sistership **Leicestershire** she was soon sold to Typaldos Brothers of Greece who converted her for use on the overnight ferry service to Crete under the new name of **Chania**, as which **Warwickshire** sailed from Liverpool on 13 April bound for Piraeus. **Leicestershire**, which had left Liverpool six weeks earlier as **Heraklion**, capsized in heavy weather on 8 December 1966 off the island of Falkonera whilst on passage from Canea to Piraeus. Her cargo of lorries and cars shifted and, of the 281 persons on board, only 47 survived. The following year Typaldos Brothers went bankrupt and **Chania** was laid up at Piraeus, reportedly becoming derelict after 1971 as **Sirius** before being broken up at Aspropyrgos in 1980.

Booth Line's **Bernard** passes Battery Point at speed in order to dock at Avonmouth very late on the ebb tide of 1 July 1967. Built by Wm Pickersgill at Sunderland in 1952 as **Siddons** for Lamport & Holt, she took the name **Rubens** in 1955 before becoming **Bernard** in 1965 for the duration of a bareboat charter to Booth. Subsequently, loading at Porto Alegre in August 1967 for Lamport & Holt, she was soon renamed **Rossini** until being transferred to Booth Line in 1970 and reverting to the name **Bernard**. Sold by the Vestey Group in 1973 to the mysterious Sopac Bulk Carriers with a charter back to Booth Line and renamed **Berwell Adventure**, she was repossessed by Booth in July 1974, doubtless due to non payment of the purchase price. Soon sold to Abbas Gokal's Gulf Shipping Group and renamed **Al Turab**, she was first reported as such sailing from Bayonne on 2 September 1974 bound for Saigon and finally arrived at Gadani Beach on 16 December 1977 to be broken up.

Sailing from Avonmouth on 31 March 1966 is Johnston Warren Lines' **Rowanmore**, built by Harland & Wolff at Glasgow in 1956. While Furness Withy & Company, which also controlled Prince Line, Cairn Line and Manchester Liners, had created Johnston Warren Lines in 1934, trading areas were becoming blurred and fleet replacement in the mid-1950s was, it seems, allocated to these different companies for tax rather than operational reasons. Between 1958 and 1960, **Rowanmore** was chartered out to Brocklebank Line as **Madulsima** and in 1971 was transferred to Pacific Steam Navigation Company, sporting their yellow funnel, for the remainder of her Furness Withy Group ownership. Sold to Greece in 1973, she traded as **Andriana I** until 1977 and then as **Marjorie Y** until finally arriving at Gandia, Spain, on 3 December 1979 to be broken up. In 1980, the Furness Withy Group was sold to the Hong Kong based shipowner C Y Tung who, concentrating on building up Orient Overseas Container Line, soon disposed of the old ships and in 1990 sold his Furness Withy interests to Rudolf A Oetker, operator of Hamburg South America Line (Hamburg Süd), also a growing container operator, which now serves the traditional Furness Withy trading areas.

Guinea Gulf Line's **Elizabeth Holt** arrives at Avonmouth on 28 January 1965 from Pointe Noire in West Africa. One of a pair built in 1953 by Cammell Laird at Birkenhead, the other being **Florence Holt**, she was soon to be sold to Greek owners. John Holt & Co of Liverpool, longstanding traders to West Africa, had created Guinea Gulf Line in 1954 but, with political unrest in West Africa in the early 1960s, and it seems preparing for an exit from shipowning, formed a limited company of that name in 1962 and soon passed the ship management to T & J Brocklebank. Later in 1965 Guinea Gulf Line Limited was sold to rivals Elder Dempster Lines Limited who retained the fleet's identity but sold the ships which were replaced by their own tonnage. Purchased by Mark Scufalos of Greece, **Elizabeth Holt** was briefly named **Admiralty Crest** before becoming **Despina N** and then, shortly before being sold for breaking in 1973, renamed **Lorain** as which she arrived at Kaohsiung on 21 October that year. **Florence Holt** was similarly renamed **Admiralty Flyer** and then **Trias**. Under this name she was laid up in a poor condition at Rotterdam in 1973 and eventually made her way to Kaohsiung for breaking as **Mr Norman**.

Sailing from Avonmouth on 27 September 1966 is Prince Line's **Cyprian Prince**, operating on a cargo liner service from the eastern Mediterranean. Prince Line was founded in 1884 by James Knott of Newcastle. All three of his sons being killed in the First World War, Sir James Knott sold his company at the end of 1916 to Furness Withy & Co. During the late 1950s and early 1960s, flag discrimination and subsidised foreign tonnage forced a contraction of services and Prince Line thereafter concentrated on Mediterranean routes, ordering two cellular container ships in 1979. Furness Withy management then amalgamated Prince Line with Manchester Liners in order to combine sailings from Ellesmere Port and Felixstowe. **Cyprian Prince**, built in 1949 at

Burntisland, was sold early in 1967 to the London Greek P A Lemos and Associates who renamed her **Agios Dionisios**, soon trading her as far as the USA and Australia until selling her in 1972. Renamed **Irene's Wish**, and then in 1973 **Fulmar Trader** after purchase by John Yannios, during a voyage from Spezia to Lagos she suffered a fire in the engine room when off Cartagena on 10 January 1976. She was towed into Palma Bay where the fire was extinguished a week later. Declared a constructive total loss for insurance purposes, it was the intention to take her to Piraeus for repair but on 14 February she sank off Palermo during the tow to Greece.

Approaching Avonmouth from Philadelphia on 10 February 1973 is **London Banker** on her last voyage for London & Overseas Freighters (LOF). Built in 1963 in Holland, and followed into the LOF fleet by four similar ships, **London Banker** was sold on 26 February 1973 to Mina Corporation (T Tricoglou) of Greece. As **Riva** she was laid up at Galaxidi on 7 May 1982, finally making a single loaded voyage to Kandla as **Alysia Bay** in May 1986 before being beached at Fouzderhat in Chittagong on 20 August 1986 to be broken up. LOF, created in 1949 by Rethymnis & Kulukundis to operate tankers, initially operated ten dry cargo ships transferred from Counties Ship Management Limited, a company they had started in 1936 and operated separately until 1970. Manuel Kulukundis, whose Kasos-based family had long been involved in tramp shipping, had in 1921 along with his cousin, Minas Rethymnis, started business together in London as Rethymnis & Kulukundis Limited. By 1927 they were joined by two Kulukundis brothers and cousin Basil Mavroleon, purchasing their first ship in 1934. In 1955 Mavroleon formed a separate company, named Mavroleon Brothers, which in 1961 had taken delivery of **Finnamore Valley**, a forerunner to **London Banker**, built at the same Dutch yard. In 1972, LOF had started to modernise its dry cargo fleet with four SD14s built by its Austin & Pickersgill subsidiary, followed in 1977 by bulk carriers, but all were sold by 1982 and the company thereafter operated only a small number of tankers until 1996 when the Swedish Frontline Shipping took control.

Akassa Palm, built for Palm Line in 1958 at Vegesack near Bremen, was photographed on 21 October 1970 from Avonmouth's south pier at the end of a voyage from West Africa. William Hesketh Lever, soapmaker at Port Sunlight near Bromborough, had in 1916 acquired the Manchester firm of Herbert Watson & Company, renaming it Bromport Steamship, to carry raw material such as palm kernel from West Africa. In 1923, Bromport was absorbed into Lever's Niger Company which, at around the time of Unilever's creation in 1929, merged with the African & Eastern Trade Corporation to become the United Africa Company Limited (UAC). After the war it was decided that UAC's ship owning should be separated from trading and so Palm Line was formed in 1949. In 1985 Unilever sold Palm Line to Elder Dempster Lines, owned by Ocean Transport and Trading who in 1989 sold its West African focused shipping business to Delmas Vieljeux. **Akassa Palm** was sold in 1972 to Thenamaris of Greece and renamed **Elenma**, passing in 1977 to Catapola Shipping who traded her as **Ionian Sky** until 1981. Purchased by Christodoulos P Kavadas, his business was already in trouble and, as **Magdalini K**, she was arrested at Aqaba in October 1982, sailing two years later for breakers near Karachi and beached on 27 November 1984. Sistership **Andoni Palm** was also purchased by Catapola, direct from Palm Line in 1976. Renamed **Mastro Manolis** she traded uneventfully until scrapped in 1982.

Chapman & Willan's 1960-built *Clearton* passes Portishead on 2 March 1967, inbound from Vancouver with a cargo of timber. She had sailed from Chemainus on 21 December, calling at Port Alberni on 8 January. The penultimate ship in a series of seven ships built by Short Bros at Sunderland, *Clearton* was soon sold to the Greek shipowners Lemos Brothers, becoming *Captain Lemos* in 1968, *Michael Angelos* in 1973 and *Kallimachos* in 1976. Sold in 1979 to the newly established Greek operator Dimitris Marinis, she continued to trade as *Sami* until sold to Pakistan breakers at Gadani Beach near Karachi where she was beached on 8 April 1982. Chapman & Willan, a Newcastle tramp ship operator essentially created in 1896, was sold in 1974 to the Burnett SS Company which had been purchased by Fednav of Canada in 1969.

F C Strick's **Muristan**, built by John Readhead at South Shields in 1950, was photographed slowly passing Battery Point on 7 August 1965 inward for Avonmouth from Bahrain. Best known for its cargo liner services between the United Kingdom and Persian/Arabian Gulf ports, Strick Line was effectively founded in 1892 by Frank C Strick, of Swansea. **Muristan** was one of seven magnificent post-war steamships, noteworthy in subsequently having their funnels heightened, presumably to allow more efficient expulsion of engine exhaust. Sold to the Greek shipowner A Halcoussis in 1966, she traded as **Leonis** for two years until becoming **Atlas Trader** and, in 1970, **Yaling** as which she arrived at Kaohsiung on 17 May 1972 to be broken up. While Strick Line had ever since 1919 been part-owned by P&O, it was only in 1972 that P&O took control. By 1975 the Strick Line fleet was fully integrated into P&O's "Strath Services" and the last Strick Line ship was sold in 1979.

Bank Line ships were infrequent visitors to Avonmouth, such calls usually being when on voyage charter to other lines but sometimes with full cargoes of ore concentrates from Australia or the Pacific Islands. *Cloverbank*, built in 1957 by Harland & Wolff at Belfast, had loaded such a cargo at Port Pirie, sailing from there on 18 June 1970, her arrival at Avonmouth being delayed by a dock strike until 3 August when we see her slowly passing Portishead. Then sold to PIL (Pacific International Lines) of Singapore, she sailed on 19 September under new colours and flag but, strangely, without change of name. Soon renamed *Kota Rakyat*, she served PIL for over a decade until broken up near Karachi where she was beached on 28 December 1981. Andrew Weir (who later became

Lord Inverforth) had started business in 1885 with a sailing ship named *Willowbank*. For several decades pursuing a policy of planned fleet replacement contracted with British shipbuilding yards, Bank Line's last such order was placed in 1977 at the site of Wm Doxford's yard in Sunderland. Bank Line's final order, for six vessels of the "Fish" Class, was completed in 1979 and the yard later closed, the ships being sold in the 1980s. Bank Line's round-the-world cargo liner service, starting at Hull and visiting South Pacific ports was retonnaged in 1996 with four former Soviet ships with roll-on/roll-off capability. Sold to the Swire Group in 2003, the service was discontinued in 2009.

Memorably docking at Avonmouth late on the ebb tide of 8 March 1964 was Manchester Liners' 1935-built **Manchester Port**. Rarely calling at Avonmouth, and this being on one of her last transatlantic voyages, the ship fortunately arrived between the snow showers. Built by Blythswood Shipbuilding at Glasgow, she arrived at Bilbao on 22 December 1964 to be broken up. Following the opening of the Manchester Ship Canal in 1894, making it possible for large ocean-going ships to sail directly into the heart of Manchester, Sir Christopher Furness, of Furness Withy & Company, had proposed in 1897 that a Manchester-based shipping line should be formed. The public prospectus for Manchester Liners Limited was issued on 10 May 1898 and Furness Withy became the largest shareholder. Manchester Liners decided from the outset to make Canada their prime route, with a secondary route to the southern United States cotton ports. By the late 1960s rising costs, strikes and restrictive practices on both sides of the Atlantic, plus subsidised competition from American shipping lines, persuaded Manchester Liners to invest in containerships. In 1981 they joined forces with Dart and Canadian Pacific on the North Atlantic. The last ship with a Manchester Liners name was the 1991-built **Francop**, chartered from new as **Manchester Trader** for one year before the operation was merged into Hamburg Süd.

Arthur Albright, passing Battery Point on 12 May 1968 with a cargo of phosphate rock from Boca Grande (Florida), had been purpose-built at Burntisland, Scotland, in 1960 to fit the dimensions of the lock into Portishead Dock where Albright & Wilson had from 1953 to 1968 operated a plant extracting molten phosphorous from imported phosphate rock. Albright and Wilson was founded at Birmingham in 1856 as a manufacturer of potassium chlorate and white phosphorus for the match industry. After processing was switched to St. John's, Newfoundland, in 1968, the phosphorus was received in two specially-built tankers until operations at Portishead ended in 1989. **Arthur Albright** traded for Empros Lines of Greece as **Avance** from 1968 until resold in 1983 to become **M Sycoutris**, owned by Loutra Shipping. After sailing from Alexandria on 29 July 1984 for Chittagong, she suffered engine trouble and ran aground near the Arabian Gulf but was refloated and towed into Ajman in 1986 but arrested and eventually sold to breakers, arriving at Gadani Beach on 25 January 1988 as **Bunny**.

Jalamanjari, photographed on 20 February 1970 from Avonmouth's south pier, was sailing from the port on a voyage which had started at Bombay on 30 December, bound for Gdansk in Poland to load a return cargo for Madras. Built in 1956 as **Meudon** for Cie de Nav d'Orbigny of La Rochelle, she was the last of ten 13 knot cargo liners built in France between 1947 and 1956 to a pre-war Wm Gray design. Scindia had in 1964 purchased all four of the latest ships in the series, *Jalamanjari* replacing a Liberty ship of the same name. Sold by Scindia in 1971 to Greek operators who renamed her **Harilion**, she suffered engine damage in October 1971 on a voyage from Hallstavik to Saigon and was towed into Abidjan and then, after discharge of her cargo, on to Marseille anchorage in August 1972. She proceeded from there to Kartal, near Istanbul, two months later to be broken up. The majority of Scindia's ships were given names prefixed Jala, meaning "water". The creation of Scindia at Bombay in 1919 by Walchand Hirachand was linked with the Swadeshi policy of boycott and non co-operation with foreign states and companies. Following Indian independence in 1947, and financially supported by the Indian government, Scindia commenced scheduled cargo liner services to the UK and USA, taking delivery of many new and secondhand ships during the 1950s. During the 1960s, the Scindia fleet and its services were further expanded but, following the global slump in the 1980s, the line ceased trading.

Passing Portishead at speed on 1 December 1973, **State of Meghalaya** was inward bound to Avonmouth, having sailed from Calcutta on 23 October. One of a large series built at Warnemünde in East Germany during the 1970s, the **State of Meghalaya** was of the Ozean type with a service speed of 16.5 knots. She was completed on 26 May 1972 as the French **Orphee** but almost immediately purchased by the Shipping Corporation of India (SCI). Warnowwerft had earlier the same year

delivered two sisterships to Scindia and both Indian lines went on to order improved Indik and Meridian type ships. **State of Meghalaya** had a particularly short existence, arriving at Bombay for the final time on 24 June 1986 to be broken up. SCI had been established at Bombay in 1961 by merging the Western and Eastern Shipping Corporations, both founded in 1950. SCI is now a diversified company with just a small presence in container services from India with five ships.

Indian Exporter, photographed on 1 October 1971 from Avonmouth's north pier, was bound for Belfast and Gothenburg on a voyage which had started at Bombay on 17 July. Built at Portland (Oregon) in 1945 as **Temple Victory**, she was one of six 15.5 knot Victory-type ships purchased in 1947 from the United States government by India Steamship (ISS) of Calcutta. ISS, its origins going back to 1928, was established as a company in the 1950s but withdrew from cargo liner operations in the early 1990s. ISS currently operates seven tankers with names prefixed "*Ratna*" reflecting its merger with the Ratnakar Shipping Company in 1989. **Indian Exporter** was soon sold to other Calcutta-based operators, Pent-Ocean Steamships, and renamed **Samudra Usha** as which she traded locally until broken up at Bombay in August 1977.

Passing Portishead on 1 May 1966, outbound from Avonmouth on a voyage from Beira to Glasgow, is **S.A. Seafarer**, her name having recently been abbreviated from **South African Seafarer** by her owners, the South African Marine Corporation Limited (Safmarine). Built at Greenock in 1950 as **Clan Shaw** and renamed **Steenbok** in 1959 before purchase by Safmarine, she was wrecked at Green Point, Table Bay, on her next outward voyage two months later, on 1 July 1966. Safmarine was created in 1946 by Dr Hendrik van der Bijl, a South African industrialist, together with States Marine Corporation of New York. **South African Seafarer** was one of three former Clan Line ships acquired by Safmarine in 1961 on purchasing the Springbok Shipping Company which

had been created in 1959 by British & Commonwealth Shipping Limited, itself created only in 1956 when Clan Line joined with the Union Castle Line, King Line and Bullard King & Company. Bullard, King & Company Limited, operators of the Natal Direct Line, which had become a subsidiary of Union Castle during World War One, had between 1956 and 1959 acquired a number of ships from Clan Line, the last being **Clan Sinclair** which was immediately transferred to the new Springbok Shipping Company and renamed **Bosbok**. Sistership **Clan Robertson** briefly operated for Bullard, King & Company as **Umzinto** before becoming **Rooibok**. These two ships then became **S.A. Statesman** and **S.A. Shipper** respectively.

King Jaja, outbound from Avonmouth on the afternoon of 23 September 1967 during a voyage from Victoria (now Limbé), Cameroon, was owned by Nigerian National Shipping Lines (NNSL) and had a service speed of 12 knots. NNSL was formed in 1957 with 33% of the capital held by the Elder Dempster Line, 16% by Palm Line and 51% by the Nigerian government. It began operations in 1959 with the acquisition of three vessels including ***Tyria*** from Anchor Line, which became ***King Jaja***. In 1961 the Nigerian government bought out the British lines and by 1974 had grown the fleet to a total of 15 vessels. In 1977 the government ordered the construction of 19 new vessels to replace the aging fleet and by 1979 the company had 24 oceangoing ships. However, after a long period of mismanagement, NNSL was liquidated in September 1995 after its remaining vessels were seized and sold. ***King Jaja***, built in 1955 by Wm Doxford at Sunderland, was sold to Greek interests at the end of 1975 and handed over at Liverpool, trading as ***Esperos*** until sold for breaking in 1978. She arrived at Gadani Beach for that purpose on 1 June 1978.

Photographed sailing from Avonmouth on 31 March 1965 bound for Rostock, **Msta** had been delivered in 1945 to the USSR by Wartsila at Helsinki, Finland. I recall being closely watched through binoculars by a Soviet security official on board the ship as she passed. The second of thirty-one timber carriers of the Khasan type built between 1945 and 1955, **Msta** was operated by the Baltic Shipping Company of Leningrad until 1955 when she was passed to the Murmansk Shipping Company who modernised the ship. Passing to the Latvian Shipping Company in 1969, it is reported that **Msta** voyaged to Lobito, Angola in 1972 and was renamed **Zutis** before being hulked in Latvia in 1975. The hulk was broken up in 1990.

Adhara, sailing from Avonmouth on 15 March 1968, was a fascinating ship to make a single voyage from India to United Kingdom ports. Owned by the Bulgarian government, she had sailed from Veraval on 27 December 1967, suffering engine trouble in January as she slowly made her way via the Cape of Good Hope to Avonmouth and Hull. She had attempted to dock immediately on arrival in the Bristol Channel on 11 March but was obliged to remain outside until a berth became available. It is believed that her bagged oilcake cargo was heavily infested with rats. Built at Odense in 1938 as *Laura Maersk* and delivered to A P Møller in February 1939, this twin screw 15 knot motorship had been seized by the United States Navy in 1941 and then operated by American President Lines as *Daystar* until the end of World War Two. Returned to her Danish owners in 1946, she served Maersk Line until 1963 when sold to Greek owners and renamed *Aeolian*. The Bulgarian government acquired the ship in 1965 but traded her as *Transrodopi II* under the nominal ownership of Transrodopi SA of Geneva until renaming her *Adhara* as this voyage commenced. Loading at Antwerp for Varna in April 1968, she later sailed from that port in October 1969 as *Kanaris*, owned by the Greek operator Vassos Haji Ioannou (Alassia SS) who soon sold her on to China and she arrived at Whampoa in November 1971 for intended demolition.

Bernhard Bästlein was a 15 knot "X" type vessel built for the East German state shipping company VEB Deutsche Seereederei (DSR) by Warnowwerft at Warnemünde near Rostock. She was launched on 30 January 1965 and completed on 30 June 1965. Photographed sailing from Avonmouth late on the morning tide of 9 September 1966, when little more than one year old, **Bernhard Bästlein** had left Chittagong on 19 July, loading bagged oilseed at the Indian port of Kakinada, sailing from there on 5 August. In 1986 this ship's name was shortened to

Bernhard for the delivery voyage to breakers at Shanghai. DSR was created on 1 July 1952 and had commenced a substantial deep sea fleet expansion programme in 1957 with several secondhand purchases and newbuildings. In 1963 DSR entered the cargo liner trades between Europe and the Indian subcontinent as a "non-conference" operator with a sailing to India of the **Dresden**. DSR ships were therefore frequently seen at Avonmouth in the 1960s and 1970s. **Dresden** is now the museum ship **Frieden** berthed at Warnemünde.

The USSR's **Professor Buznik** is seen arriving at Avonmouth on 21 February 1987, thirteen years after the end of the decade on which this book focuses, yet now considered just as historic. One of a large series built for the Soviet Union at Kherson on the River Dnieper, **Professor Buznik** was completed on 9 April 1973 and served the Black Sea Shipping Company of Odessa until sold to breakers ten years after being photographed, having been beached at Chittagong on 30 March 1997. **Professor Buznik** is an example of a design known as the Slavyansk type. In total, 31 examples were built between 1967 and 1973. Cargo gear varied. The first few were equipped with ten 5-ton cranes and later examples had five 8-ton cranes. The last ten in the series, of which this vessel is an example, were given six 8-ton cranes and also a 60-ton heavy lift derrick. The Black Sea Shipping Company, founded in 1833, had retained its identity during the Soviet era from 1917 to 1991, emerging as the privately-owned BLASCO but suffering a financial collapse in 1995 which led to the sale of its fleet of 300 ships. The 17 knot **Professor Buznik**, which had sailed from Qinhuangdao in China on 15 January 1987, had brought a cargo of oilseed for the production of animal feed, a trade which was important business for Avonmouth and provided employment for many old vessels including, during the 1990s, ships of the former Soviet Union.

Polish Ocean Lines' *Warynski* was a ship of much historic interest. Passing Portishead on 17 December 1969, she was on a voyage from Port Sudan to Gdynia via Avonmouth loaded with a cargo of bagged oilseed for animal feed. Built by Deutsche Werft, Hamburg, in 1936 as *Athen* for Deutsche Levante Linie, she was taken over by the German Navy in September 1940 and renamed *Sperrbrecher 2* as which she was mined and broke in two at Boulogne on 22 September 1940. Returned to her owners in November 1942, she was repaired, reverting to the name *Athen* in 1944. On 3 May 1945 at Neustadt, in the Lübecker Bucht, *Athen* was one of three ships loaded with refugees hit in a tragic air raid. Undamaged herself, there was heavy loss of life on the other ships and memorials on the island of Poel and at Haffkrug were established to commemorate the incident. *Athen* was acquired by the Soviet Union as part of war reparations and was renamed *General Brusilov*. In 1947 the ship was transferred to Poland and renamed *Warynski*, operated by Gdynia America Shipping Lines. She was hulked for storage in the second quarter of 1970 and broken up at Szczecin in 1973.

Kapitan Kosko, seen late in the afternoon of 6 January 1970 inbound for Avonmouth, had been built at Gdansk in 1957 as one of a large series of fine cargo liners from Polish shipyards in the 1950s. Usually termed the B54 type, they were known to Polish Ocean Lines staff as the "tenners", as they were of approximately 10,000 deadweight tonnes. In 1951 the Polish government reconstructed its shipping industry, creating Polish Ocean Lines largely out of Gdynia America Shipping Lines. Polish Ocean Lines grew to become an important worldwide cargo liner operator with services from northern Europe to and from destinations including the Far East, Indian subcontinent, Africa, Australia and South America. A long period of contraction started in the 1970s with the Polish government, in reaction to containerisation of the industry, streamlining its organisation, in 1982 replacing Polish Ocean Lines with a new corporate identity. *Kapitan Kosko* was one of many ships sold as the streamlining progressed, arriving at Hong Kong on 12 January 1979 to be broken up.

The **Seyhan**, owned by the Turkish government, was photographed from steps at the end of Avonmouth's south pier as she departed on 20 July 1974. **Seyhan** was built at Fredrikstad, Norway, in 1950 for Wallem & Company A/S of Bergen as **Norviken** and purchased by D B Deniz Nakliyati in 1955. Wallem also had an operation in Hong Kong which, as Wallem Ship Management Limited, grew rapidly following its creation in 1971. Although there have always been many small Turkish shipowners, the government set up the national shipping line D B Deniz Nakliyati TAS (Turkish Cargo Lines) in 1955, with the participation of Denizcilik Bankasi which had separately operated the ferries. The company, which had purchased several secondhand ships including **Seyhan** and embarked on a newbuilding programme, was privatised in 2000. **Seyhan** was beached at Aliaga on 15 September 1979 to be broken up.

Arriving at Avonmouth on the sunny morning of 5 September 1966 is *Ravnefjell*, owned by Olsen & Ugelstad of Oslo, Norway. Built at Kiel in 1955 for the Fjell-Oranje Line, the newly combined European Great Lakes service operated jointly by Olsen & Ugelstad and the Dutch-owned Oranje Line, *Ravnefjell* had in 1959 been lengthened by twelve metres to ninety metres overall. *Ravnefjell* was sold in 1967 to Vernicos-Eugenides who traded her as *Arta* until sold in 1980 to Uni-Ocean Lines to Singapore to become *Pacific Mulia* as which she finally arrived at Kaohsiung on 4 July 1985 to be broken up.

Also arriving at Avonmouth on 5 September 1966 is **Sunmont**, owned by Olaf Pedersen of Oslo, Norway, and on long term charter to Saguenay Terminals of Montreal, a company controlled by the Aluminium Company of Canada. Built at Kiel in 1953 as **Bow Canada** for Oivind Lorentzen of Oslo, she was in 1955 renamed **Nopal Express** but sold in 1957 to Compagnie Maritime Belge who traded her as **Liege** until 1964. It seems that she was purchased, together with sistership **Sunclipper**, by Olaf Pedersen specifically for charter to Saguenay. When the charter finished in 1967 she was given their own name of **Sunny Lady**. Sold in 1969 to Liberian flag operators, she was renamed **First Lady** in 1970 and then

Avra in 1972 before a resale to Taiwan interests. As **Golden Queen** she was soon sold by Char Ching Marine to local breakers, arriving at Kaohsiung on 7 December 1973. Saguenay had commenced operations in 1937 and the "Sun" naming policy was adopted from 1947 after a competition between employees. Using mainly chartered ships, a triangular service was established between Canada and the UK/North Europe, then to the Caribbean and finally back to Canada with bauxite for aluminium production, but operations ceased in the second half of the 1970s.

The Liberty ship **Kostis** passes Portishead, outbound from Avonmouth, on 8 June 1967 after discharging a part cargo of grain. Unfortunately, one year later, on 3 June 1968, early into a voyage from Sfax to China with a cargo of phosphate rock, **Kostis** suffered a fire, was abandoned, grounded and declared a constructive total loss. Delivered by Todd-Houston in 1944 as **Anna H Branch** and operated by the Norwegian owners Lorentzen from 1947 to 1955 as **Arthur Stove**, she had traded as **Kostis** for the London Greek Laimos Brothers since 1955. She was powered by a 3-cylinder triple expansion engine made by the Iron Fireman Manufacturing company in Portland (Oregon).

Lefkipos, passing Portishead on 3 April 1968 outbound from Avonmouth, was on a voyage charter to Anchor Line. She had sailed from Bombay on 5 January bound for Avonmouth, Liverpool and Glasgow via Karachi and Kandla where she loaded crushed bones for discharge at Cardiff. *Lefkipos* was a pre-war standard Doxford-type built at Sunderland in 1936 as *Wearpool* for Sir R Ropner & Co which had been founded at West Hartlepool in 1870. Launched on 9 June 1936, *Wearpool* was completed in just two months. Sold by Ropner in 1954 to Ragnar Källström of Sweden, she traded until 1964 as *Adelso*, primarily for the carriage of iron ore from the Swedish ports of Luleå and Oxelösund. Purchased in 1964 by the Greek domiciled Union Commercial SS Co (Mark Scufalos), *Lefkipos* was renamed *Dimitros* in 1971. She arrived at La Spezia in October 1979 to be broken up after a period of inactivity in the Piraeus district in the spring of 1975, followed by long term lay-up.

Marian's voyage to Avonmouth which had started at Karachi on 15 November 1973, with calls at Cape Town on 4 January and St Vincent (CV) on 25 January, was something of an epic. Loading a cargo of bulk animal feed at Kandla between 16 November and 10 December, she suffered machinery problems which slowed her progress to such an extent that her agent had booked tugs and labour two weeks before her arrival on 9 February 1974, unaware that she had only just sailed from the Cape Verde Islands off West Africa. On completion of discharge, *Marian* was detained due to deficiencies including a rusted load line which was repainted while the ship lay alongside the repair jetty in Avonmouth's Old Dock. While fog had descended on the port the previous day, when she was booked to sail, her eventual sailing day of 14 March was clear and sunny. The photographs depict the ship moving out of the Old Dock and then departing from the Royal Edward lock bound for Oslo, where she arrived on 22 March, to discharge the remainder of her cargo.

Marian was built at Sunderland by Wm Pickersgill, launched on 9 November 1953 and delivered in March 1954 as *Ramon De Larrinaga* to the Liverpool-based owner Larrinaga Steamship, created in 1931 by a long established family with Basque origins. Sold to N Leondaras and P Kallikis of Greece in 1969 and renamed *Marianna*, her name was shortened to *Marian* on transfer to the Cypriot flag in 1972. *Marian* later suffered two incidents at Lisbon. In December 1974 she put into the port with engine damage and had to be towed from there to Rotterdam for repairs; a year later *Marian* again put into Lisbon with engine trouble, this time with a cargo of cement loaded at Rostock for the Arabian Gulf. On sailing, with the cargo reportedly having solidified, she grounded outside Lisbon on 26 March 1976; although refloated, she sank under tow 13 miles off Cabo Raso the following day.

Passing Portishead, outbound from Avonmouth, on 12 September 1964 after discharging a part cargo of timber from British Columbia, is the Greek-owned Liberty ship **Archangelos** which had sailed from Vancouver on 30 June, calling at Los Angeles on 28 July. Built at Panama City in 1943 as **Dolly Madison**, she was one of a number of war-built ships operated by Atalanti M Livanos, who had purchased her in 1950. Just two months later, on 15 November 1964, she sprang a leak and sank off Baja California on a voyage from Philadelphia to Tokyo with a cargo of scrap metal.

Passing close to Battery Point as she approached Avonmouth on 29 April 1964 on a loaded voyage from British Columbia is the Greek-owned Liberty ship **Aristotelis**. Built at Houston in 1943 as **John W Gates**, she was one of a number of war-built ships sold to Greece when the war ended, continuously trading for Aristotelis S Onassis from 1946 until arriving at Onomichi, Japan, in October 1968 to be broken up.

The Panamanian-flagged **Nunez De Balboa** made a splendid sight slowly passing Portishead on the afternoon of 23 October 1966 bound for Avonmouth with a cargo of sulphur, probably loaded at Beaumont in Texas. She was built in 1942 at the J L Thompson yard in Sunderland. Delivered to Albyn Line (Allan, Black, & Co, of Sunderland) as **Thistlemuir** and owned since 1961 by Adolfo Ramirez Escudero of Bilbao, Spain, **Nunez De Balboa** was soon sold for breaking, arriving at Osaka in May 1968 for that purpose. In 1956, the same owner had purchased the **Mooncrest**, built by Lithgows in 1941, trading her as **Kori** for fourteen years until sending her to breakers in 1970.

The Liberian-flagged **Portalon** passes Portishead on 5 March 1967 bound for Avonmouth with a part cargo of grain from South America. She was built in 1947 at the Wm Denny shipyard in Dumbarton. Delivered to Australind SS (Trinder, Anderson) as **Australind** and owned since 1959 by Eduardo De Aznar of Bilbao, Spain, manager of the well-known Naviera Aznar SA, **Portalon** was laid up at Bilbao in 1971 and eventually towed to Santander for breaking, work starting on 13 March 1972. In 1886 Trinder, Anderson & Co had joined Charles Bethell to start a steamer service called the West Australian Steam Navigation Company, their first ship being named **Australind**. In 1904 Bethell, Gwyn and Trinder, Anderson together formed the Australind Steam Shipping Company. Trinder, Anderson & Company had strong connections with the Federal Steam Navigation Company and the New Zealand Shipping Company from 1954 managing the ships operated by the Avenue Shipping Company. Bethell, Gwyn had started business in Corn Street, Bristol, in 1898, moving to Baldwin Street, until they followed most other agents to Avonmouth in 1973. Bethell, Gwyn were from 1964 wholly owned by the P&O group and therefore handled all P&O Group ships, including Federal, in addition to T & J Harrison and Henderson Line.

A/B Transmarin (Transatlantic Marine), founded by Bernhard Ingelsson at Helsingborg, Sweden, in 1916, had for many decades provided a regular service from Scandinavia to Bristol City Docks. The company's **Becky**, built at Gothenburg in 1945, had in fact been sold in 1965 to John E Sandstrom of Stockholm, placed under the Panamanian flag and chartered back, at least until 30 March 1967 when seen passing Portishead inbound for Bristol. The charter ending soon afterwards, **Becky** commenced to trade away from northern Europe. Sold in 1975 to

Greek buyers associated with the fast growing Flandermar Shipping Company and renamed **Ellitsa**, she continued to trade worldwide until arriving at Koper in July 1976. Thereafter remaining in the Mediterranean area, she was acquired by fellow Greeks Moriatis Shipping in 1980 who sailed the ship to Freetown only for her to be laid up and abandoned to local interests who were going to trade her as **Timbu** until she suffered a fire on 28 January 1981 and was consequently broken up.

Bermuda Hibiscus, a modified "standard fast cargo liner" built by Lithgows at Port Glasgow in 1946 for the Canadian Pacific Railway Co as **Beaverglen**, was operating for Persian Shipping Services, a trading name used by Iranian Lloyd, of Teheran. Photographed passing Portishead, slowly approaching Avonmouth, on 20 September 1964, her outward voyage was from Glasgow on 8 May 1964 to Dammam where she had arrived on 3 August, having suffered boiler trouble en route. Nominally owned since 1963 by Hibiscus Limited, of Bermuda, but still registered in London, she was sold early in 1965. As **Ping An**, owned by Teh Hu Steamship of Hong Kong, she was almost immediately wrecked five nautical miles north of the Hook of Holland on 24 November 1965 while undergoing engine trials and was broken up in situ.

Victoria was built at Gothenburg in 1930 as ***Vasaholm*** for Swedish America Line. She was a regular visitor to Portishead Dock with cargoes of phosphate rock from Florida and was photographed passing Battery Point on 31 August 1964. In 1944 employed in the Mediterranean as a Swedish Red Cross relief ship, she was purchased in 1954 by O M Thore who traded her as ***Victoria*** until sold to Greece in 1965 and renamed ***Stavros***. After arriving at Piraeus on 14 March 1966 for repairs, she emerged early in 1967 as ***Priamos*** as which she continued trading until beached at Istanbul on 7 March 1973 to be broken up.

Arriving at Avonmouth on 23 September 1972 from East Africa on the short-lived Alpha Lines cargo liner service, **Aegis Power** was operated by Aegis Shipping, a fast-growing concern owned by N D Papalios of Athens whose family had started business in 1949 but entered liquidation in 1985. Built by Vickers Armstrong at Newcastle in 1954 as **Pacific Northwest** for Furness, Withy & Co, along with several other former British cargo liners, she was purchased by Papalios to trade as **Aegis Power** from mid-1971 until arriving at Shanghai on 3 April 1974 to be broken up. Furness Withy & Co was created in 1891 when the Furness Line was merged with the business of Edward Withy and Company, largely trading to New York and subsequently, to the Pacific coast of the USA and Canada.

Master Nicos was photographed on 28 March 1969 together with **Renwick**, a coal barge converted for sand dredging. Outward bound from Avonmouth for Hull after discharging a part cargo loaded at Bombay, and built at Tamise in Belgium in 1964 for Phocean Ship Agency (Michael N Eustathiou), **Master Nicos** was the last of a series of similar ships built at various European yards for the same owners since 1955. Sold to N Dacoronias in 1980, she traded as **Irene D** until beached at Alang on 29 June 1984 to be broken up.

Around 1890, Thomas Wilton had joined with a Mr Renwick, who managed a household coal business in Torquay. By 1951 they were joined by Fredrick C Dobson to become Renwick, Wilton & Dobson Limited as which they also set up business as coal contractors at Bristol and Newport, operating **Renwick** and other barges in the Bristol Channel until selling out to Thomas Silvey. **Renwick**, ordered from J R Hepworth of Hull and delivered in 1951, was retained in the Silvey fleet and in 1967 converted at Saul for sand dredging. Later operating as **Sand Opal** for Sand Supplies (Western) Limited, a subsidiary of Thomas Silvey, she was sold to South Coast owners in 1976 and renamed **Sargia**.

Elders & Fyffes' 18 knot *Chirripo* is seen passing Battery Point at speed on 7 May 1966, inbound from Avonmouth with bananas from San Antonio, Jamaica, from where she had sailed on 27 April. It is recorded that the "banana boats" were known as the 'plum' boats because they offered overtime to the casual dock workers and were also liked by customs officials for their hospitality. Elders & Fyffes was established in 1901 as a subsidiary of Elder Dempster of Liverpool with the London fruit distributors Fyffe, Hudson & Company supplying working capital. The Bristol stevedoring and towage company C J King and Sons contributed a stake, receiving in return contracts to handle the discharge of fruit and the supply of tugs. In the 1920s, the United Fruit Company of New York had acquired a controlling interest in the company. Built by Alexander Stephen at Linthouse, Glasgow, in 1957, *Chirripo* was transferred in 1969 to United Fruit's subsidiary Honduran company, trading as *Olancho* until sold to Greece in 1972 and renamed *Mardina Exporter* as which she arrived at Kaohsiung on 6 June 1974 to be broken up.

Also arriving at Avonmouth on the morning tide of 5 September 1966 was the **Calamares** of Caraibische Scheepvaart Maats. She was built by Cammell Laird at Birkenhead in 1956 and had accommodation for twelve passengers. Created by United Fruit in 1956 as a joint venture with managers Van Nievelt, Goudriaan, the Caraibische Scheepvaart Maats (Caribbean Shipping Company) had started business with **Calamares** and her sisterships **Cartago** and **Carillo** and went on during 1969/71 to have eleven United Fruit vessels transferred to its nominal ownership. All fourteen ships were disposed of between 1975 and 1977, **Calamares** being transferred in 1977 to United Fruit's Honduran subsidiary company before being sold to Taiwan breakers, arriving at Kaohsiung on 7 January 1979.

Arriving at Avonmouth on the ebb tide of 21 September 1965 is the molasses tanker **Athelduke**. Built by Sir John Laing's shipyard at Sunderland in 1949, she was the second of two sisterships built at the yard for Athel Line of Liverpool. The tanker arrived at Hirao, south of Hiroshima, Japan, on 6 June 1967 to be broken up. Athel Line Limited came into being in January 1940 as a wholly-owned subsidiary of United Molasses to own and operate the group's tanker fleet. In 1965, United Molasses was taken over by Tate & Lyle. The last Athel Line ships, **Athelmonarch** and **Athelqueen**, built in 1977, were sold in 1980.

Constructed by Furness Shipbuilding at Haverton Hill, Teesside in 1959 for John I Jacobs, it would seem that **Regent Falcon**, photographed passing Portishead on 4 September 1965, was built specifically for a long-term time charter to the Regent Oil Company. In 1971 her managers became Texaco Overseas Tankship Limited and her name was changed the following year to **Texaco Durham**. Sold to Greece in 1975, the ship traded for Eletson Maritime Services as **Kalliopolis** until arriving at Gadani Beach near Karachi on 1 December 1982 to be broken up. Trinidad leaseholds had launched the Regent brand of petrol in 1930 and the Regent Oil Company was created in 1948 to market both Regent and Caltex in the UK. Expanding in the 1950s into shipping and refining, Regent Petroleum Tankship Company was created in 1956 but the name disappeared after Texaco took control in 1967.

One of a series of tankers constructed in UK and German yards in the late 1950s and early 1960s for the Royal Dutch Shell Group, *Achatina*, built at Vegesack near Bremen in 1958, passes Portishead on 19 November 1969. *Achatina* was transferred in 1982 from her original nominal owners, Tanker Finance Limited, created in 1957, to Shell Tankers (UK) Limited but was soon sold for breaking, being beached at Chittagong on 29 August 1984. The Royal Dutch Shell Group was created in February 1907 through the merger of two rival companies which had started business in the 1890s, NV Koninklijke Nederlandsche Petroleum Maatschappij and the "Shell" Transport and Trading Company Ltd, the name of Shell deriving from the business of importing and selling sea shells. In 1921, following Shell's acquisition of the Mexican Eagle Petroleum Company in 1919, Shell-Mex Limited was formed to market products under both the "Shell" and "Eagle" brands, from 1932 in cooperation with BP to become Shell-Mex and BP Limited, which separated in 1975.

Making her way out of Avonmouth past Battery Point in a strong westerly wind on 20 September 1968 is **British Trust**, an early example of the eleven 1959/62 "Bird Class" of BP tankers, albeit the only one not given the name of a bird. **British Trust**, launched by Dame Patti Menzies, wife of the Australian Prime Minister Sir Robert Menzies, may have originally been intended to be named **British Kiwi**. It is surmised that, as the Kiwi is the national emblem of New Zealand, it was politic to give the ship a less controversial name. A sistership named **British Kiwi** was delivered in January 1960. Completed by Lithgows at Port Glasgow in October

1959 the **British Trust**, along with all but the last two of her sisterships, was delivered to the newly-formed Clyde Charter Company Limited. Transferred to the BP Tanker Company Limited in 1972, she was sold in 1976 along with three sisterships to China and placed under the management of the Ocean Tramping Company Limited of Hong Kong. Renamed **Tingjiang** (sisterships **British Gannet** became **Hanjiang**, **British Kestrel** became **Sunjiang** and **British Curlew** became **Wenjiang**), she was absorbed into the mainland Chinese fleet in 1979 as **Da Qing 235** and broken up locally in 1995.

Lowland Tankers had been created in 1951 as a joint venture between British Petroleum, Matheson of Hong Kong and Common Brothers of Newcastle who managed the fleet. By 1965, this fleet comprised fifteen ships built between 1953 and 1962. **Border Laird**, built by Lithgows at Port Glasgow in 1955, was photographed sailing from Avonmouth on 4 November 1965. She had traded worldwide, by January 1966 being on a voyage between Japan and the Arabian Gulf, and finally arrived at Kaohsiung on 8 July 1972 to be broken up.

The tanker *Fortuity*, passing close to Portishead on the evening tide of 31 October 1971, had been built for Lowland Tankers by Scott's at Greenock in 1953 as ***Border Regiment***. Purchased in 1969 by the fast-growing Greek concern Southern Shipping & Finance, created in London in 1947 by Kedros & Hayialidis, who also purchased several of her sisterships, *Fortuity* arrived at Masan, South Korea, on 20 February 1975 to be broken up. In about 2002 the Southern Shipping and Finance operation moved to Greece and continues to thrive as ***Halkidon Shipping Corporation***.

Adolf Bratt, who had started business at Gothenburg, Sweden, in 1877, and had created his company "A/B Adolf" in 1912, had for many decades provided a regular service to Bristol City Docks importing pulp from Scandinavia. His final ship was the **Gertrud Bratt**, built at Bruges in 1957. This vessel, seen passing Portishead on 19 March 1967, continued the service together with chartered ships until the end of 1967. Managed by Erik Kekonius until January 1967, it seems that **Gertrud Bratt** had together with A/B Adolf then been acquired by Salénrederierna. Purchased in November 1967 by Martinez, Pereira y Cia SA, of Valparaiso, Chile, and renamed **Carmen**, she traded in the Pacific for ten years until grounding and being wrecked off Tapolobampo, Mexico, on 12 October 1977 during a loaded voyage from Mazatlan to Guaymas.

The red-hulled ships owned by the Danish owner J Lauritzen, who had started business at Copenhagen in 1884, were well-known at Bristol City Docks and on occasions called at Avonmouth. The **Thora Dan** was built by H C Stülcken Sohn at Hamburg in 1956. She passes Portishead on 20 March 1967 outbound from Avonmouth, probably on a voyage from Canada. **Thora Dan** was sold in 1974 to D Kosmas, C Karafotias and E Karelias of Greece who had started business together two years earlier,

subsequently building up a large fleet, including three other former "*Dan*" ships but suffering a number of casualties, as a result of which they soon ceased business. The **Thora Dan** had traded as **Elias K** until, on a loaded voyage from Kakinada to Rotterdam, she arrived at Madras on 4 November 1977 under tow after suffering an engine room fire. She was eventually beached at Bombay on 31 January 1979 to be broken up. J Lauritzen is now a major operator of bulk carriers.

Stalheim was photographed sailing past Avonmouth's south pier, outbound from Bristol City Docks to Oslo, on 26 March 1965 with Portishead power station ahead. One of a pair of new ships, the other being **Stanford**, built at Lekkerkerk in 1959 for J B Stang, a company formed in 1906 and linked with Fearnley & Eger of Oslo, she and her predecessors had been regular visitors to Bristol from Scandinavia with cargoes such as woodpulp. Remarkably, **Stalheim** survived until 2010, largely trading in the Mediterranean as **Mudistar** from 1972, **Pardi** from 1979, **Sonita** from 1994 until finally as the Turkish-owned **A Asli** from 1998 until being beached at Aliaga on 24 December 2010 to be broken up. **Stanford** meanwhile disappeared off the coast of Vietnam in 1988 as **Lucky Star**.

The Greek-owned **Georgios Roussos**, passing Avonmouth's south pier bound for Bristol City Docks with a deck cargo of timber on 17 October 1964, was a fascinating old ship built in 1922 at Grabow in the German port of Stettin as **Ophelia**. Sold to a Flensburg company in 1930 and renamed **Mildburg**, she ran aground on Öland Island, Sweden, in 1931, was declared a total loss and sold at auction to Rederi A/B Monark of Stockholm. Renamed **Montrose** in 1933, she was sold in 1938 to Ingolf N Schander of Elleholm, near Karlshamn, and renamed **Rita** but re-purchased by Monark in 1958, reverting to the name **Montrose**. Sold to Roussos Bros of Piraeus early in 1964, she traded as **Georgios Roussos** until beached on 3 June 1966 off Cape Matapan, the southernmost point of mainland Greece, after springing a leak during a voyage from Izmir to Helsingborg with cottonseed. She was then broken up.

Launched on 21 August 1949 and delivered in January 1950, the locally well-known the **Pluto** was one of a series built by Charles Hill to Bristol Steam Navigation's own specifications. She is seen passing Portishead in February 1967 on a routine but possible final voyage from Irish or northern continental ports to Bristol, a service which had commenced in 1821 and concluded by the end of the 1970s on amalgamating with Bristol Seaway Limited and the Irish services of Seawheel Limited. Sold to Agenzia Marittima Duodo of Venice and renamed **Dino**, she foundered off Capo Teulada, Sardinia, on 9 April 1973 on a voyage between Sant'Antioco, from where she had just sailed, and Porto Marghera (Venice) with a cargo of clay.

Salcombe, passing close to Battery Point on 17 June 1965 at the start of a regular passage from Portishead to Newport to load another cargo of coal, had been purchased secondhand by Osborn & Wallis in 1941 from the Newcastle Coal and Shipping Company. Osborn & Wallis, who had started business in Bristol in 1880, sold their last two ships in 1970 to W E Dowds of Newport while Portishead's coal fired power station finally closed in 1976. Built in 1938 at Lekkerkerk as **Camroux IV**, **Salcombe** was sold in 1969, trading as **Friars Craig** until, after three changes of ownership, being scuttled in 1985 as an artificial reef off Barbados.

The **Kentish Coast** was photographed on 2 May 1966 as she passed Pill on the River Avon outbound from Bristol on one of her last voyages, the inward leg being from Bordeaux to Liverpool and Glasgow. Launched on 16 May 1946 as **Ulster Duchess** for the Belfast Steamship Company, she was between 1947 and 1954 transferred to Coast Lines service as **Jersey Coast** before reverting to Belfast SS as **Ulster Weaver** for ten years until becoming **Kentish Coast**. Sold in 1968 to Kuwaiti interests she traded for several years, including at first to northern Europe, as **Salimiah Coast**. Her ultimate fate is unknown. Coast Lines, formed in 1913, was purchased in 1917 by Lord Kylsant's Royal Mail Group, subsequently acquiring Belfast SS and Burns & Laird. Regaining its independence in 1935, Coast Lines was sold to P&O in 1971. This photograph was taken on the return journey to Portishead after seeing **Dunera** sail from Avonmouth.

The **Michael M** was built at Westerbroek in 1955. We see her outbound from Bristol on 23 April 1968 and was unusually photographed in process of disembarking her pilot to the **Nancy Raymond** off Battery Point. Sold to Lebanese interests in 1974, sailing from Rotterdam as **Sliema** in March 1975, she was soon renamed **Imad**, then sold to Syria in 1979 becoming **Lucky Wish**, in 1980 **Khalil I** and in 1987 **Princess Fatimah** as which she possibly continued trading until 2009. Metcalf Motor Coasters, started in 1924 by Thomas J Metcalf, was acquired by Bookers in 1972, following which their S William Coe & Company Limited and Metcalf Motor Coasters Limited merged in 1978 as Coe Metcalf Shipping then sold to Fishers of Barrow in 1984, becoming James Fisher & Sons (Liverpool) Limited in 1995.

Yewdale passes Battery Point, outbound from Avonmouth, in May 1967. John Stewart & Company, formed at Glasgow in 1910, had operated the coaster from delivery in 1949 by James Lamont at Port Glasgow until sale in 1969 to the Konstantinidis family of Greece. Renamed ***Sanaga***, and managed by Dalex Shipping Company (G Dalacouras) of Piraeus, she grounded on 28 March 1971 and was wrecked off Pointe des Chats, on the south-east of Ile de Groix near Lorient, on a ballast voyage from Plymouth to St Nazaire. John Stewart ceased operations in 1991.

General Steam Navigation's **Crane** is the earliest photograph in this book, taken on 24 February 1964 as she passed Pill on the River Avon outbound from Bristol on one of her last voyages, the inward leg being from Bordeaux to Liverpool and Glasgow. The ferry service between Pill and Shirehampton was a convenient short cut when travelling between Portishead and Avonmouth by public transport, albeit at low water passengers were obliged to walk along a muddy slipway for much of the distance. A group of London businessmen had set up the General Steam Navigation Company in 1824. Largely serving the near-continental trades and Mediterranean, the line's success led to its acquisition in 1920 by P&O who, respecting that success, had very little involvement in GSN's management until the mid-1960s when its routes were being challenged by the roll-on/roll-off ferry and the container ship. In October 1971, GSN's fleet was merged with the former Coast Lines operations as P&O Short Sea Shipping which became P&O Ferries. Built at Troon in 1937, **Crane** was sold to Greece later in 1964, trading as **Nissos Sifnos** until 1969 and then as **Toula** until 1975. Kuwait owners then traded her as **Al Madani** until 1981 when she was reportedly broken up as **Gulf Ace**.

The **Seamew** was another vessel in the fleet of the General Steam Navigation Company. A twin screw vessel, she was built in 1947 at the S P Austin yard in Sunderland. Here she passes Avonmouth's south pier bound for Bristol City Docks on 21 September 1965. Together with sisterships **Auk** and **Laverock**, **Seamew** was built for trading to Iberia. **Seamew** was sold in 1966 to Adamantios & Mikes Bousses of Piraeus and renamed **Marigo**. As such she was an occasional visitor to Avonmouth and we see her thus in the next photograph. Resold in 1972 to Kavadas Bros and renamed **Capetan Chronis**, on 3 June 1974, en route from Benghazi to Piraeus in ballast, she was sunk in a collision north of Tolmeta, Libya.

Marigo, the former **Seamew**, passes Portishead, inbound for Avonmouth, in early March 1967. Sistership **Auk**, also sold to Greece in 1965, after five years in lay up at Port Said from 1977 as **Ouranoupolis**, spent ten years in the Great Bitter Lake before being towed back to Port Said for breaking on April 1992. The former **Laverock** fared better, trading as **Chania II** until broken up at Murcia in May 1980.

F T Everard's coastal tanker **Alchymist**, built by A & J Inglis at Glasgow in 1945 for war service as **Empire Orkney** and purchased by Everard in 1949, was photographed passing close to Battery Point dodging the ebb tide on 30 September 1964. She arrived at Bruges on 3 May 1969 to be broken up. The Everard company was founded in 1889 by Frederick T Everard, a builder of Thames sailing barges with a works at Greenhithe in Kent, subsequently building a large and well-known fleet of coastal dry cargo ships and tankers until, at end of 2006, the company was sold to James Fisher PLC.

Well-known and easily recognisable on the Bristol Channel in the 1950s and 1960s was F T Everard's *Acclivity*. She was built for the Athel Line as *Atheltarn* at the Birkenhead yard of Cammell Laird in 1929. She sailed for South Africa to serve the molasses trade centred around Durban but, due to poor market conditions returned to the UK in 1931. Purchased by Everard in 1952, *Acclivity* arrived at Boom, south of Antwerp, on 4 May 1966 to be broken up. We see her sailing from Avonmouth on 21 September 1965.

Built by Charles Hill at Bristol in 1952 for the local operation of the Regent Oil Company, **Regent Jane** passes Portishead on 3 January 1966 in company with a Dutch coaster which had together taken the first lock of the tide out of Avonmouth, dodging the fast incoming tide by sailing close inshore. Lengthened by fifteen and a half feet by Charles Hill in July-October 1961, she was sold in 1967 to Celtic Coasters of Dublin and in 1968 renamed **Breeda J**. As such she was broken up at Passage West in September 1975. Regent Oil had operated storage facilities at Avonmouth and had built a refinery at Milford Haven in 1962.

Also built by Charles Hill at Bristol in 1952 for the local operation of the Regent Oil Company, **Regent Robin** was photographed rounding the north pier at Avonmouth after leaving the first lock of the tide bound for Gloucester on 5 September 1966. Laid up at the end of 1966 when Regent stopped supplying their depot at Stourport-on-Severn, she was converted at Sharpness into a sand dredger by Douglas Arnold and in 1970 was renamed **Sand Robin**. As such she was owned in Bedhampton on the Solent. In 1999 she was sold again and was reported to have been converted back to a tanker and renamed **Regent Linnet**.

Wyesdale H passes Portishead on 13 December 1964 in tandem with *British Maple*. Built in 1952 for John Harker by Sharpness Shipyard, the tanker was one of a large number of small craft built for operating on the River Severn. *Wyesdale H* had been modified at Gloucester in 1961, being given a raised forecastle, to allow trading to Swansea. Hazardous weather and tidal conditions have contributed to many accidents close to the old Severn railway bridge that linked Sharpness and Lydney, the most serious being on the night of 25 October 1960 when *Wyesdale H* came close to becoming a third casualty along with *Arkendale H* and sistership *Wastdale H* in which five crew members lost their lives. *Wyesdale H* was sold later in the 1960s to Southern Tanker & Bunkering at Southampton and renamed *Easternstan*. In 1970 she was acquired by a Crawley-based company to become *Bagshot* and in 1975 was renamed *Aquator*. She is believed to have been scrapped at Rochester in 1986.

Built by Charles Hill at Bristol in 1950 for the local operation of the Holms Sand & Gravel (T R Brown), the sand suction dredger **Steep Holm** was photographed passing close to Battery Point on 21 February 1966 outbound from Bristol. Sadly, on 2 October 1968, **Steep Holm** was wrecked on Tusker Rock near Porthcawl when bound for Swansea loaded with sand. The descendants of Thomas Robert Brown, who started business at Chepstow in the 1870s, had created Holms Sand & Gravel in 1924 and a Liverpool-based operation Norwest Sand & Ballast Company in 1955. The Bristol operation closed in the late 1980s and the Company's last ship, the 1961 Bristol-built **Norstar**, was broken up in Clarence Dock, Liverpool, during 2003.

Bristol Sand & Gravel Company's suction dredger **Camerton** was built at Troon in 1950. She was photographed on 9 September 1964 passing Portishead outbound from Bristol to load sand in the Bristol Channel. Bristol Sand & Gravel Company, which had started business in 1920, was acquired by the British Dredging Group in 1966 and **Camerton** continued to operate locally in new colours until sold to Greece in 1973. However, as **Archonto** she traded for little more than a year, being broken up at Lavrion, south of Athens, in April 1974.

The suction dredger **B.D. 10** sails past Avonmouth's south pier, outbound from Avonmouth's Old Dock, on 26 March 1965. In order to free the name for a new ship, this former **S.D. Severn** had only recently been renamed after serving the Port of Bristol Authority continuously from delivery in 1919 by William Simons of Renfrew. The Corporation of Bristol (City Council) had taken over the operation of Bristol's City Docks from private ownership in 1848, later managing them by a Committee of the Corporation acting under the title of "The Bristol Port Authority". Avonmouth and Portishead Docks were acquired in 1884 and their operations combined with the City Docks under the Port of Bristol Authority umbrella. In 1966, when the new **S.D. Severn** came into service, **B.D. 10** was sold for breaking at Newport. "B.D." logically stands for "*Bristol Dredger*". The first, **B.D. No.1**, was delivered to the PBA in 1886.

The dredger **B.D. Clifton**, built at Paisley in 1925 as **Clifton**, also sails past Avonmouth's south pier, outbound from Avonmouth's Old Dock, on 10 November 1967. The industrial activity at Portishead can clearly be seen in the distance with the Albright & Wilson phosphorus works to the left and the power stations with four chimney stacks behind **B.D. Clifton**'s superstructure. Portishead "A" power station was closed in 1976, its two chimney stacks being demolished in 1981/2 while Portishead "B" power station closed in 1982, its stacks being demolished in October 1992. Soon sold for breaking, **B.D. Clifton** arrived at Briton Ferry on 12 August 1968 for that purpose.

The mud hopper **Avon**, built by Charles Hill at Bristol in 1956, sails past Avonmouth's south pier, the red and white pennants indicating bound for Avonmouth's Old Dock. Together with sistership **Frome**, the **Avon** was sold in 1980 to Northwood (Fareham) Limited, then in 1986 to Govan Davies Developments Limited and was broken up at Milford Haven in May 1993. **Avon** or **Frome** could often be seen in Bristol's Cumberland Basin alongside the bucket dredger **Samuel Plimsoll**.

It was relatively uncommon in the 1960s for Avonmouth-based tugs to venture past Battery Point to meet incoming ships, it being more usual to wait for late running ships off Portishead Dock entrance. C J King's **Bristolian** was built at Leith in 1911. She is seen here passing Battery Point on 22 April 1965. Christopher King, a master stevedore, had acquired his first steam tug, **Merrimac**, in 1859. In 1899 his sons set up the Alarm Steam Tug Company Limited, the first of King's strategically designated one-ship companies. **Bristolian** was consequently owned by the Bristolian Steam Tug Company Limited. Her working life over, in 1967 she was offered to the City Council to be a working museum vessel but as the City Docks were still active commercially, the offer was declined and she was sold for demolition at Newport in 1968.

The Sharpness pilot boat, waiting off Portishead for an incoming ship on 11 July 1972, had started life in 1933 as the **Always Ready**, built at Cowes to serve as the Runswick Lifeboat. After her coxswain had died of injuries received when trying to save a lad's life alongside the salvage boat **Disperser** during a northerly gale in February 1934, she had the name Robert Patton added and was thereafter known as **Robert Patton the Always Ready**. Purchased by Bridgwater pilots in 1953, she was converted into a pilot boat at Kimber's boatyard at Highbridge but soon resold to Sharpness pilots and renamed **Alaska**, the name of an old Gloucester sailing cutter, carrying out 8,394 acts as a pilot boat between November 1956 and March 1974 before being retired, Gloucester/Sharpness pilots then sharing the Bristol boat at the eastern station. Still to be seen in the Bristol Channel as **Alaska One**, she had been purchased in 1978 by Craig Glassonbury and brought back to pristine condition by R W Davis & Son at Saul, Gloucester, being used as often as possible for cruising and raising funds for the RNLI.

The Bristol Port Authority's own tug, **Cabot**, built by Charles Hill at Bristol in 1952, was photographed leaving Avonmouth in the first lock of the tide incoming on 28 February 1968 in company with **Pengarth** and ahead of her, a British Waterways tug bound for Sharpness with a barge in tow. Not often seen in the river, **Cabot** was sold in 1974 to Maritime Towing & Salvage of London, and in 1982 to Winnie Towing of Lowestoft, before being purchased later in the 1980s by B Murphy of Eire who broke her up at Oldcourt near Cork in 1995.

In this aerial view on 2 January 1965 by F G Warne of an impressively full but idle Avonmouth Docks, looking towards Portishead, ships are double banked along West Wharf. **Gloucester City**, which had arrived on 30 December from Baltimore, can just be seen on the opposite side of the dock with sistership **New York City**, which had suffered a collision on her voyage from Detroit, repairing on the North Wall at the end of West Wharf. There are two large tankers, **Polyclipper** which had docked on New Year's Day from Baton Rouge and **Alexander Maersk** which sailed later on 2 January to Curaçao, in the oil basin plus two coastal tankers including Everard's **Acclivity** and a Harker barge on the move. The ships alongside West Wharf (WW) are as follows: Nearest, on WW3, **Jalagouri** which had arrived on 20 December from Calcutta with Comben Longstaff's **Chesterbook**, which had arrived from Bayonne on 2 January with a cargo of sulphur, alongside - probably waiting for WW4. On WW2 the **Broland**, which had arrived on Christmas Eve from Port Angeles, with either **Halifax City** or **Montreal City** (both had arrived on 31 December) alongside her. On WW1, Royal Mail Line's **Loch Loyal**, which had arrived on 30 December from Vancouver, with **Indian Exporter**, one of India SS "Victory" ships, which had docked on new year's day from Calcutta, alongside her. **Clan Graham**, which had arrived from Beira on 23 December, is berthed on T Shed, adjacent to the entrance lock, with Saguenay Terminals' **Sunseahorse**, which had arrived on Christmas Day from Halifax, on S Shed and the East German **Leipzig**, which had arrived on Boxing Day from Calcutta, alongside R Shed.